40 DAYS FOR LIFE DEVOTIONAL

THE 40 DAY JOURNEY THROUGH THE LIFE OF CHRIST

KOLBE & ANTHONY
PUBLISHING

DAY 1

Intention:
For mothers facing unexpected pregnancies.

Scripture:
"Then the angel said to her, 'Do not be afraid, Mary, for you have found favor with God. Behold, you will conceive in your womb and bear a son, and you shall name him Jesus.'"
—*Luke 1:30-33*

Reflection:
Mary faced the most unexpected pregnancy of all. When the angel appeared to her, she was given a choice to accept a singular role as the mother of the savior of the world. Within an instant she said yes to God, and the moment she did, the eternal entered the temporal.

Since the fall of Adam and Eve, our Lord had been preparing for this day when his son would enter human history as a newborn child. Christ could have been born to any queen in the land—into any mighty, wealthy, or powerful family. Instead, God chose a humble, unwed teenage mother.

In so doing, God wove Christ's birth into the story of every unexpected pregnancy. When Mary encountered the angel Gabriel, she didn't plan to be a mother, but she freely accepted this calling. From the minute Mary declared, "May it be done to me according to your word," until the hour she stood at the foot of the cross, her entire life was oriented to her son. She existed to serve him, and through her willingness to fulfill God's will, she gave humanity the greatest gift of all time—God's only begotten son, love incarnate, the word made flesh.

Every life is a reflection of God's love. Expectant mothers facing unplanned pregnancies often experience deeply challenging circumstances—worry about how they will care for their babies, pressure from family members to abort, and concerns about the future they will be able to provide for their children, among a host of other challenges. Yet just as God sent the angel Gabriel to Mary, he makes his presence known to mothers facing difficulties.

"Women experiencing an unplanned pregnancy also deserve unplanned joy," said Emmy Award-winning actress Patricia Heaton. Though the hardships, doubts, and uncertainties are real, so too is the grace that God gives to every new parent. Bringing a child into this world is a sacrificial choice. It is a chance to give of ourselves for a child who is a part of us. Let us pray that every woman chooses life for her child—the greatest gift she can give and receive.

Prayer:

God, we ask you to be with every expectant mother. Give them the courage of Mary to say yes to your divine will, even in the most unexpected circumstances. Help us to notice women in need and embrace every mother facing an unplanned pregnancy. Amen.

Day 2

Intention:

For fathers to have the courage of Joseph.

Scripture:

"When Joseph awoke, he did as the angel of the Lord had commanded him and took his wife into his home." —*Matthew 1:24*

Reflection:

When Joseph first heard the news that Mary was "with child," he knew that he would become the subject of ridicule, gossip, scandal, and humiliation for taking her as his wife. Yet when the angel of the Lord appeared to him in a dream, Joseph immediately accepted God's will, even if he didn't fully understand the divine conception.

Men often face their own difficult "Joseph moments" when they learn that they are going to become fathers. Fears race to the surface—fears of not being ready, of not having an adequate job or home for a baby. Men often fear they will make the same mistakes their own fathers made and fail to be present for their children.

Although these fears are legitimate, men do not have to carry the responsibility of fatherhood alone. Even in the darkest moments, Christ is with us. When we place our trust in God, he gives us the grace to face the unknown.

New fathers also need holy men to strengthen them on their journey. Proverbs 27:17 reminds us, "Iron is sharpened by iron; one person sharpens another."

For the men participating in this 40 Days for Life campaign: I encourage you to pray about whether God is calling you to find ways to mentor and support young men in your community. We need more men of faith to encourage young dads to be present in their children's lives and lead their families with boldness.

Through our prayers and mentorship, God will give new fathers the courage of Joseph.

Prayer:

Lord, thank you for the example of Joseph, who shows us what it means to live with courage in the wake of fear and uncertainty. Bless all fathers with the strength of Joseph so that in every circumstance they may place their trust in you. Help all fathers to answer the call of sacrificial love that comes with the birth of every child. Give them the strength to be not afraid. Amen.

DAY 3

Intention:

For couples suffering from infertility.

Scripture:

"But the angel said to him, 'Do not be afraid, Zechariah, because your prayer has been heard. Your wife Elizabeth will bear you a son, and you shall name him John. ... He will be filled with the Holy Spirit even from his mother's womb, and he will turn many of the children of Israel to the Lord their God.'"
—*Luke 1:13,15-16*

Reflection:

Every couple who has struggled with infertility can find hope in the story of Elizabeth and Zechariah.

In the ancient Jewish culture, the pain of barrenness was compounded by shame and social isolation. Such an affliction was considered to be a sign that God did not grant his favor upon that household. But Elizabeth's infertility was not a failure or a punishment from God. Her life was full of purpose.

Elizabeth and Zechariah lived holy lives even before John entered their family. Elizabeth must have served many neighbors, relatives, and friends with her motherly heart, and Zechariah served God and his Jewish brothers and sisters through his faithfulness as a priest.

Saint Josemaría Escrivá, a Spanish priest who encouraged all Christians to seek holiness in the middle of the world, was once asked how couples should bear the pain of infertility. He said: "God in his providence has two ways of blessing marriages: one by giving them children; and the other, sometimes, because he loves them so much, by not giving them children. I don't know which is the better blessing."

Christ makes all things new, and he is capable of transforming infertility into a gift of self—even if that new life does not conform to our expectations or the world's norms.

Such a trial is certainly a mystery. As St. Josemaría explained, "Often God does not give children because he is asking them for something more. ... God is urging them to make their lives a generous Christian service, a different apostolate from the one they would have fulfilled with their children, but an equally marvelous one. God, who always rewards, will fill with a deep joy those souls who have had the generous humility of not thinking of themselves."

We can all accompany couples pained by infertility by affirming their lives as beautiful witnesses to God's love, which transcends familial ties and expands the hearts of every person who accepts his grace.

Prayer:

Our Father in heaven, we pray in a special way for all those who struggle with infertility. We ask you to give them peace in their suffering, strength in their perseverance, and healing in body and soul. In the midst of sorrow and uncertainty, fill them with your joy so that, as Romans promises, they "may abound in hope by the power of the Holy Spirit." We ask this in Jesus's name. Amen.

DAY 4

Intention:

For parents to experience the joy of every child, including those with disabilities.

Scripture:

"And how does this happen to me, that the mother of my Lord should come to me? For at the moment the sound of your greeting reached my ears, the infant in my womb leaped for joy." —*Luke 1:43-44*

Reflection:

Few things are more central to the Christian life and the human experience than the simple yet powerful disposition of joy. As the English writer and Christian apologist G.K. Chesterton wrote, "Joy...is the gigantic secret of the Christian." It is an outpouring of the peace we find in Christ.

Even before Christ was born, he brought joy to others. As soon as Elizabeth heard her cousin Mary approaching, the baby in her womb "leaped for joy."

Science has now proven that babies in the womb can respond to different sensations from the outside world. For example, unborn children can hear and react to music, recognize the voices of their mothers, and feel their mothers' emotions. This is a testament to the joy that unborn children and their families can experience even before birth.

Sadly, some doctors push parents to abort if they detect that a child may have a disability. It is estimated that between 60 to 90 percent of children diagnosed with Down syndrome are aborted. Not only is this a grave injustice to the child, but it robs families of the person God has called them to love.

As countless parents have attested, children with disabilities are a source of joy unlike any other. Research shows that individuals with Down syndrome, for instance, are overwhelmingly happy—and parents of children with Down syndrome have highly positive outlooks on life.

In his 2017 testimony before Congress, Frank Stephens embodied this joy: "I am a man with Down syndrome—and my life is worth living," Stephens said.

"Seriously, I have a great life! I have lectured at universities, acted in an award-winning film and an Emmy-winning TV show, and spoken to thousands of young people about the value of inclusion in making America great."

Anyone who has had the chance to get to know someone with a disability has witnessed firsthand that they see the world in ways in which the rest of us cannot. They have gifts that are unique and irreplaceable. They remind us in a special way that every life brings joy to the world and that each child is created in the image and likeness of God.

Prayer:

Lord, help us renew our gratitude for the joy that each child brings into our lives. We ask you to bless, keep, and cause your face to shine upon all unborn children—especially those with disabilities. Give parents supernatural strength and overwhelming support from their community to care for their child with special needs. Amen.

DAY 5

Intention:

For the friends and families of expectant mothers.

Scripture:

"Her neighbors and relatives heard that the Lord had shown his great mercy toward her, and they rejoiced with her." —*Luke 1:58*

Reflection:

Elizabeth's friends must have stood by her side throughout the pain of infertility, the happy surprise of her pregnancy, and her first days of motherhood. Through friendship, we are called to serve each other and share in our joys and sorrows. This accompaniment makes real the compassion of Christ.

Many expectant mothers feel alone and afraid, particularly if a family member or partner is pressuring them to seek an abortion. Through the work of so many churches, crisis pregnancy centers, and personal initiatives, we have an opportunity to support expectant mothers in the tender months of pregnancy and early parenting. This can take many forms, from hosting baby showers to bringing meals to being a steadfast friend and source of encouragement.

God leads us to the mothers and fathers he is asking us to serve. By being the hands and feet of Christ to expectant mothers, we can doubly affirm the gift of life. We love both woman and child when we care for new mothers.

Just as Elizabeth's friends and relatives stood by her side, we are called to love our neighbors and serve the vulnerable. Sometimes the smallest actions make the most profound difference: a kind word, a helping hand, or a listening ear. This is true friendship: to seek what is best for the other person at all times.

Through friendship we can change the life of a mother and child, and our lives will also be forever changed.

Prayer:

Dear Lord, thank you for the gift of friendship. Teach us to see your beauty in those around us, and give us the grace to serve our friends and neighbors. We ask you to especially bless the families and friends of expectant mothers. Help those who are close to expectant mothers to offer the compassionate care that Elizabeth's friends did throughout her pregnancy. Help us never to close our eyes to women in need. Amen.

DAY 6

Intention:

That every child may reach his or her God-given purpose.

Scripture:

"All who heard these things took them to heart, saying, 'What, then, will this child be?' For surely the hand of the Lord was with him." —*Luke 1:66*

Reflection:

With the news of every unborn child comes an outpouring of emotions: anticipation, excitement, and at times anxiety about the future. Is my baby healthy? What will my child love to do? What will he or she grow up to be? These are questions every expectant parent wonders.

The birth of John the Baptist reminds us of the anticipation that accompanies the birth of every new child. After nine months of being mute, Zechariah obeyed the angel's command to name his son John. Immediately thereafter, his "tongue [was] freed" and he "spoke blessing God."

This news of God's miracle led people to ask, "What, then, will this child be?"

Elizabeth and Zechariah must have pondered the same question as any new parent does. For families facing hardships, this question becomes even more pressing. Yet John's birth reminds us that God has a unique plan for every child.

No baby is a mistake. No life is an accident. Every child is created by God with a noble purpose, and each life changes the world.

As children grow up, some may wonder if they are wanted or if they will amount to anything. We must pray all children know they are loved by God and that their lives have meaning. When a child knows he is loved, he can do anything. He can walk with the confidence that someone cares for him. How much greater is our heavenly Father's love for us? Let us place our fears in his hands.

Prayer:

Lord, instill confidence and hope in every child. Help all children to grow up to see the purpose for which you made them. Give parents the wisdom and understanding to see the needs of each child and to nurture each child's talents for your glory alone. Amen.

DAY 7

Intention:
For mothers and babies in need of a safe place to stay.

Scripture:
"While they were there, the time came for her to have her child, and she gave birth to her firstborn son. She wrapped him in swaddling clothes and laid him in a manger, because there was no room for them in the inn."
—*Luke 2:6-7*

Reflection:
Imagine how Mary and Joseph must have felt when they arrived in Bethlehem. They had traveled a long distance as Mary endured the final days of pregnancy. Upon arriving in Bethlehem, they could not find a single place to stay.

Hospitality was an important custom for the Israelites, who had been instructed by God to extend generosity to others out of gratitude for God's care for them (Leviticus 19:33-34). But Mary and Joseph did not receive that hospitality as they searched for a place to give birth to the son of God.

The inns were full. The workers were busy. Mary and Joseph were turned away until one person had mercy on them, offering them a lowly stable. Like the poor widow of the Gospel who gave her last two coins in the temple, the owner could not give much, but he gave Mary and Joseph all he had.

It was a humbling birth for the savior of the world, who was laid in a manger instead of a crib. Even though this was almost certainly not the birth that Mary and Joseph imagined, God entered into the unexpected. Through the birth of his son, God can use the most unglamorous situation as a chance to encounter him.

Like the owner of the stable, we can offer what we have to pregnant moms in need of safe shelter. Even when we think we don't have enough to give, God enters into these moments just as he entered into the stable on Christmas Day.

Prayer:

Dear Jesus, you entered the world through the "yes" of your mother. Help us to say "yes" to the needs of those around us, especially the needs of expectant mothers. Open our hearts so that we might generously share your love with others, and help us to be a refuge for women and children seeking safety and care. Amen.

DAY 8

Intention:

For all doctors, nurses, and health care workers to have the wisdom and strength to save the most vulnerable lives.

Scripture:

"They were overjoyed at seeing the star."
—*Matthew 2:10*

Reflection:

The three kings who followed the star to Bethlehem were truth-seekers. Also called magi, which means "magicians" or "wise men" in Latin, these men were scholars who blended astrology and natural science to discern the meanings of the stars. Even though they were not part of God's covenant with the Israelites, the magi sought the truth at all times, and their curiosity and dedication to that truth led them to an encounter with God himself.

Christ came as a vulnerable infant, and this was how the three kings first saw him. In each child, born or unborn, the image of Christ is visible. The cause of protecting life is not only a religious one; all people who seek justice and truth can come to understand the inherent dignity of life.

So many families can attest to doctors and nurses who helped save their lives through their astute medical care, and this is especially true for the smallest, most vulnerable patients: unborn children.

In a Toronto hospital in March 2022, a pair of twins, Adiah and Adrian Rajendram, were born prematurely at 21 weeks and 5 days old. They were each under one pound. Initially, doctors were not sure they would be able to resuscitate the babies because there wasn't a tube small enough, but the twins' parents prayed for a miracle. Through the careful attention of a doctor who nurtured the babies through many complications, the twins celebrated their first birthday in 2023.

In an interview with the National Catholic Register, the doctor, Prakesh Shah, said: "I find that neonatal [cases are the] ones more exciting, challenging, and rewarding, in the sense that these are the families who did not have [much of a chance] of taking a baby home."

Physicians like Dr. Shah are God's hands on earth. They give parents hope and care for those who remind us most of Jesus in the manger. They need our prayers for wisdom and discernment as they find new ways to save the most fragile lives.

Prayer:

Jesus, you are the divine physician and the source of all life. Bless doctors, nurses, and health care professionals so that they might always protect the gift of life. Help them to see you in every patient. As you heal our souls, let them heal our bodies. Amen.

DAY 9

Intention:

For lawmakers on the front lines of passing legislation to end abortion in America.

Scripture:

"When Herod realized that he had been deceived by the magi, he became furious. He ordered the massacre of all the boys in Bethlehem and its vicinity two years old and under, in accordance with the time he had ascertained from the magi." —*Matthew 2:16*

Reflection:

After the angel appeared to the magi and told them not to return to Herod, they risked their lives to protect the infant Jesus, the living son of God. The magi likely had to go to great lengths to uphold the angel's wishes and avoid being captured by Herod's men—risking their lives to protect our Lord when he was most vulnerable.

We must pray that God gives lawmakers the courage of the magi.

For nearly 50 years, people prayed and worked for the day when the Supreme Court would overturn *Roe v. Wade*. America has entered into a new chapter of hope, but the fight for life is far from over. Lawmakers at both the state and national levels now have a responsibility to pass legislation that protects the first and most fundamental right: the right to life.

Tragically, in the aftermath of the *Dobbs* decision, roughly 20 states have passed measures to maintain or expand abortion laws. Yet during that same period, we have also witnessed the most transformative action to end abortion in America: at least 25 states have passed laws to protect the lives of mothers and their unborn children.

We give thanks for the lawmakers who have courageously defended the unborn, even at the cost of their political careers. One such courageous leader is Congressman Dan Lipinski from Illinois. The only pro-life Democrat in Congress, Lipinski lost his seat in 2020 because pro-abortion groups poured millions of dollars into defeating him in the primary. In the face of such opposition, Rep. Lipinski did not waver.

"Over the years, I've watched many other politicians succumb to pressure and change their position on this issue," said Rep. Lipinski. "I have always said that I would never give up being pro-life and standing up for babies in the womb."

Just as the abolition of slavery began in our churches, Americans of faith have driven the movement to protect the unborn. We can all work to elect leaders who stand up for the most vulnerable among us. Through our prayers, work, and civic engagement, we will see the day when abortion will not only be illegal but unthinkable in America. No issue is more important than saving the lives of unborn children.

Prayer:

Lord, we pray that you bless all lawmakers with the courage of the magi. We ask that you bestow wisdom and good judgment on those who serve in government. Give them the strength to do what is right and the courage to risk their careers to protect the unborn. Help them to use their positions of authority to cherish and defend life in America. Thy will be done on earth as it is in heaven. Amen.

DAY 10

Intention:

To accept the things we cannot understand.

Scripture:

"And he said to them, 'Why were you look-ing for me? Did you not know that I must be in my Father's house?' But they did not understand what he said to them. He went down with them and came to Nazareth, and was obedient to them; and his mother kept all these things in her heart." —*Luke 2:49-51*

Reflection:

Multiple times in the Gospels, Mary ponders events in her heart, suggesting that she did not fully understand the meaning of events but knew they were from God and took them to her prayer.

The first mention of Mary's reflection comes after the shepherds visit the newborn baby Jesus and go forth to share the good news they have received from the angel. This moment is both an end and a beginning. Mary accepted God's will and carried Jesus in her womb for nine months, and her pregnancy culminated in Christ's birth, the word made flesh. She must have savored these first days with her newborn son, and after the visit of the shepherds, she ponders how this precious child will change not only her life but the whole world.

Only a few verses later, Luke tells of the holy family's visit to Jerusalem, when Mary and Joseph lose track of Jesus. "Your father and I have been looking for you with great anxiety," Mary tells him when they are reunited. Jesus had been teaching in the temple, expounding on the scriptures to the Jewish rabbis, but Mary and Joseph "did not understand what he said to them."

Suffering is one of the most difficult realities to understand. Yet it is full of meaning when united to the cross. Scottish missionary Oswald Chambers wrote, "If through a broken heart God can bring his purposes to pass in the world, then thank him for breaking your heart."

Mary was at Christ's side as he came into the world and as he left it. She knew the savior as only a mother can. Yet she still bumped up against the limits of human understanding. She shows us how to encounter things we cannot understand: Pray. Ponder in our hearts. Give all things to her son.

Prayer:

Lord, we trust that you are always with us even as we encounter the mysteries of life, both great and small. Please give us the grace to accept your will for our lives, especially in the moments when we cannot fully understand how your plan will work together for good. Give us a spirit of thanksgiving so that we might turn to you in all suffering, joy, and confusion in this world. Amen.

DAY 11

Intention:

That every mother, father, and child would experience God's loving fatherhood.

Scripture:

"And a voice came from the heavens, saying, 'This is my beloved Son, with whom I am well pleased.'" —*Matthew 3:17*

Reflection:

When Adam and Eve disobeyed in the Garden of Eden, they fell prey to the serpent's lie that God is a harsh master rather than a loving father. Adam and Eve doubted the goodness of God's laws and rejected his fatherhood by seeking their own will instead. Sin ruptured the relationship between God and man, leading to a double lie: that God does not love us for who we are and that we must earn his approval.

At Christ's baptism, God speaks from the heavens and tells the whole world of his love for his son. Jesus has not begun his public ministry; he has not earned his father's love through his deeds. Rather, God delights in Jesus simply for who he is: his beloved son.

Through baptism, we are all beloved sons and daughters of God. As individuals committed to the pro-life cause, we seek to proclaim this truth to every mother, father, and child. Yet it's a truth that's often hard for people to accept. Many people grew up in painful family circumstances—some children never heard their fathers say "I love you no matter what" or "I'm proud of you." Others only saw their fathers on occasion, and some never had the chance to meet their dads. Even great dads are imperfect, so it can be hard to fully comprehend what it means when we often say the first two words that Christ taught us to pray: our Father.

As theologian Scott Hahn has explained, "We must go beyond our earthly experiences and memories of fatherhood when we pray, 'Our Father.' For though He is a provider, begetter, and protector, God is more *unlike* than *like* any human father, patriarch, or paternal figure. … Unlike earthly fathers, He always has the best intentions for His children, and He always has the ability to carry them out. Jesus wanted us to know this, so that we could always approach our heavenly Father with childlike trust and confidence: '[W]hatever you ask in prayer, you will receive, if you have faith' (Matt 21:22)."

God is the perfect father. He will never abandon you, and he always loves you simply because he created you. He saw that it was good for you to exist, and all he wants in return is your love freely given.

Prayer:

Dear God, you are a good and gracious father. Help us to stand firm in our identity as your sons and daughters so that we might share your love with everyone we encounter. Heal the wounds caused by our shortcomings and the shortcomings of others. We pray that every parent and child might know that you love them more than anyone else in the world ever can. Amen.

DAY 12

Intention:

For the strength to resist the temptation of discouragement.

Scripture:

"Then the devil took him up to a very high mountain, and showed him all the kingdoms of the world in their magnificence, and he said to him, 'All these I shall give to you, if you will prostrate yourself and worship me.'"
—*Matthew 4:8-9*

Reflection:

Even Christ underwent temptation during his earthly ministry. When the Holy Spirit leads Jesus into the desert for forty days, Satan tries to allure Jesus with the false promises of worldly glory.

In a culture driven largely by comfort and career-building, it can be tempting to fall prey to Satan's false promises. Devoting our time, resources, and energy to standing up for life can feel like a burden too heavy to bear.

One of the greatest temptations facing us today is despair. Despair tries to convince us that we are too far gone, beyond the grasp of God himself. A heart in despair rejects the possibility of redemption. The future often lies in a cloud of obscurity, and we can project this uncertainty onto the present.

At times it's tempting to grow discouraged by the long road ahead to protect every innocent life, especially when our friends or family members hold different views. But we know that defending the unborn is always fruitful, even if we don't see the fruit in this life.

In 2018, a couple visited an abortion facility in Sacramento, California. They were homeless and unemployed, and they felt they had no choice. As the mother put on her gown and began to prepare for the terrible procedure, her husband waited outside. "We can't possibly add the responsibility of two more babies," he told a 40 Days for Life witness who talked with him. In the midst of their brief conversation, the husband quickly realized that he and his wife were making a grave mistake.

Not knowing what he would find inside, he walked into the clinic and rescued his wife right before the abortion began. Years later, the mother came back to the group of prayerful witnesses. She was holding hands with two toddlers—they were twins. "You saved my babies and my family," she said with tears in her eyes. Not one, but two beautiful children are alive today because of the gentle words of one prayer warrior.

If we call upon God's name, he will give us the strength to resist temptation and hold true the hope that we find in Christ.

Prayer:

Lord, help each of us overcome the temptation of discouragement. Give us the perseverance to follow your will and remember that you hear our prayers even when we don't see the results. If it is your will, use us to save more lives than we will know in this lifetime. Amen.

Day 13

Intention:

For scientific and medical leaders to make life-saving advancements.

Scripture:

"Amen, amen, I say to you, we speak of what we know and we testify to what we have seen, but you people do not accept our testimony. If I tell you about earthly things and you do not believe, how will you believe if I tell you about heavenly things?" —*John 3:11-12*

Reflection:

God reveals his majesty in the very atoms of our being. He has written his name into the complexities of the universe. Consider the extravagance of our creator who showers us with more gifts than we can fathom: an entire galaxy millions of miles away appears as a single pinprick of light in our sky, while a simple wildflower in a field might only ever be seen by one farmer.

In this Gospel scene, Jesus speaks to Nicodemus, a highly educated Pharisee. Nicodemus doubts Jesus not because he is ignorant, but because he doesn't want to accept the truth.

Today, many in our society are quick to use science to disprove God, but they ignore the science of life. Medical and scientific leaders need our prayers for fearless pursuit of the truth in their field.

One such scientist was the courageous Dr. Jérôme Lejeune. In the 1950s, he discovered that Down syndrome was caused by an extra copy of chromosome 21. While he used this discovery to improve the lives of Down syndrome patients, other medical experts began to use the finding to abort children who had the extra chromosome.

Even though he knew it would ruin his career, Dr. Lejeune fearlessly spoke out on behalf of the unborn. After receiving a prestigious genetics award in the United States, he implored his audience not to abuse science to end life. "For thousands of years, medicine has striven to fight for life and health against disease and death. Any reversal of this order would entirely change medicine itself," he courageously said in front of a room of renowned scientists.

Later that night, Dr. Lejeune wrote a letter to his wife: "Today I lost my Nobel Prize." His prediction came true. The scientific community condemned and ostracized him, almost certainly denying him the Nobel Prize because of his courageous defense of life.

We need more scientists like Dr. Lejeune who will make discoveries to save the most premature babies and improve the lives of those with disabilities. We ask God to give them the courage to defend the most fragile lives through their intricate knowledge of creation.

Prayer:

Creator of all things, we praise you for your magnificent creation. We seek the truth in science because we cannot help but wonder at your works. Inspire our medical and scientific leaders to pursue the truth, proclaiming the existence of life in the womb and defending it until natural death.

DAY 14

Intention:

For the courage to follow Christ's will.

Scripture:

"Jesus said to them, 'Come after me, and I will make you fishers of men.' Then they abandoned their nets and followed him."
—*Mark 1:17-18*

Reflection:

When Jesus invites his disciples to follow him, he offers them the choice to stay comfortable in their current lives or to answer the call of Christ and give up everything they know.

Christ sparks a longing within every soul. He is unlike anyone the disciples have ever met: he works miracles, he speaks truths both old and new, and he calls each of them by name.

Christ also calls each of us by name, and at times he asks us to abandon our own plans to follow his will for our lives.

God doesn't "need" us in the strict sense of the word. He is all-powerful, all-knowing, and all-present. He has existed for all time and is perfect without us. Yet he chooses to "need" us to help bring many souls to Christ.

As Catholic evangelist Bishop Robert Barron put it, "It's God who acts, and if we give ourselves to his creative power, he will make us into something far better than we ever could."

Often in the most unexpected moments, we hear Christ's call: to offer support to a struggling mother, to engage in an uncomfortable conversation with a pro-choice friend, to volunteer at a women's pregnancy center, or simply to pray for the unborn.

Listen and answer these calls, because Christ will use the smallest deeds to change the hearts and save the lives of thousands.

Prayer:

Lord, we pray that you might grant each of us the courage to follow your will, regardless of the personal cost. You made your disciples Simon and Andrew into "fishers of men" so that they could bring other people closer to you. Help us to do the same. We ask that you bless all people in the pro-life movement by reminding them that you are with them. Help them to carry out their earthly mission in a way that reflects your eternal love. Amen.

Day 15

Intention:

For the faith to believe that God will work miracles through us.

Scripture:

"His mother said to the servers, 'Do whatever he tells you.'" —*John 2:5*

Reflection:

God often speaks the loudest to us through his silence. In so many biblical scenes, major details are left missing, leaving Christians pondering the in-betweens. Just as the unspoken, implied scenes in the Bible can be the richest for contemplation, the moments of uncertainty in our own lives can be the most faith-filled.

We are often left in the dark, but we are never left without God. When situations are difficult to understand, we can see the uncertainty we face as a chance to contemplate our Lord.

At the wedding feast at Cana, Mary notices a problem: the wine has run short. Before this problem becomes a crisis—before the hosts are embarrassed and the festivities abruptly end—she brings it to her son. Jesus responds, "Woman," using a term that is both respectful and intimate, "How does your concern affect me? My hour has not yet come." How many conversations between mother and son must have been had before this? What look was exchanged between Jesus and his mother that led her to guide the servants with such confidence?

Mary does not hesitate to ask this favor on behalf of the others at the wedding. Immediately, she brings her son to the servants, confident that he will fix the problem. She does not shy away from asking for favors from Christ, and neither should we.

Jesus does not explicitly tell the servers what he is about to do. He implicitly asks them to trust his word. First, he tells them to fill the six empty wine jars with water, and they obey. Next, he tells them to draw some out to take to the head waiter. Again, without question, they do what he tells them. When the head waiter tastes the water that has been transformed into wine, he is amazed. "You have kept the good wine until now," he says.

Jesus could have spoken just one word and changed the water into wine, but he asks instead for the help of the servants. What a magnificent and humbling gift it is to be used by God. Let us strive to be instruments of God's mercy. Jesus turned water into wine. He can work miracles through us, if only we let him.

Prayer:

Lord Jesus, you have used water for wine and mud to make a blind man see. Please use me as your instrument on earth. Let others feel your compassion when I encounter them. Let your work be done through my hands. Please let me especially care for mothers and their unborn children with the faith that always desires to lead people to your side.

DAY 16

Intention:

That God will give us merciful hearts that bring healing and hope to individuals who have worked in the abortion industry.

Scripture:

"Blessed are the merciful, for they will be shown mercy. Blessed are the clean of heart, for they will see God. Blessed are the peace-makers, for they will be called children of God." —*Matthew 5:7-9*

Reflection:

Not one of us has merited the infinite mercy of God, yet it flows unceasingly to those who ask for it. When you pray for justice, pray for the justice of Christ, which is more merciful than fair. Pray for mercy, because in a just world, not one person has earned salvation. God's love is not measured, it is extravagant.

Be bold in prayer—bold in requests for God's mercy for ourselves and for others.

As Christians and as advocates for the unborn, we will not win others over through logic, science, or reason alone. The battle to protect innocent life is a battle of the heart. The mercy of Christ is not a mathematical equation; it is a grace that we do not earn or deserve. Christ asks us to show others the same mercy that he freely bestows upon us.

Dr. Anthony Levatino, a former abortion doctor, spoke of the power of the 40 Days for Life prayerful presence. "That presence is huge," he said. "You have no idea the people you're affecting, but you are. It's incredible work. Please keep doing it."

Love is persuasive. Cleanliness of heart is not merely an absence of sin. It is living in the presence of God so fully and freely that there is no room for selfishness and vice.

Only from this outpouring of love in our own lives can we show others the mercy of Christ. When we experience God's infinite mercy, our hearts expand and we grow in understanding of others, especially those who have been deeply wounded by their work in the abortion industry. Lord, give us merciful hearts.

Prayer:

Lord, in your infinite mercy, bring healing and hope to those caught in the lies of the abortion industry. Answer my prayer for forgiveness on their behalf: "Thoroughly wash away my guilt; and from my sin cleanse me." If it is your will, help me to know how to show men and women who work in abortion clinics your love, to get to know their names and their stories, to pray for them, to have an understanding heart, and to see them as you see them—as your children who have been deeply wounded by sin. Thank you for the many courageous workers who have left the industry and now save lives through their testimonies. Let them be a witness of hope for current abortion workers.

DAY 17

Intention:

For the creativity and initiative to go to extraordinary lengths to reach mothers contemplating abortions.

Scripture:

"They came bringing to him a paralytic carried by four men. Unable to get near Jesus because of the crowd, they opened up the roof above him. After they had broken through, they let down the mat on which the paralytic was lying. When Jesus saw their faith, he said to the paralytic, 'Child, your sins are forgiven.'"
—*Mark 2:3-5*

Reflection:

Consider the paralysis of a woman contemplating an abortion: a paralysis of fear, pressure, and hopelessness. It is a feeling of being trapped, alone, and having no one to turn to. Though abortion advocates consider themselves "pro-choice," we know that, in truth, most women only resort to an abortion if they feel they have no other choice. They often don't want to harm their own bodies or kill their babies, but they simply feel like they cannot mother their children.

Above all, women need to know that they are not alone. They need to know that they are worthy of exquisite care and that there are people who will support them throughout the journey. They need to know that they are free to choose life, not forced into the false choice of abortion.

The women who walk into abortion clinics often confront a cacophony of voices shouting that they are not strong enough, they are not accomplished enough, and they can't bring a new life into this world. We know this is a lie from the devil. We can help women see the truth through our gentle and open arms of support and encouragement.

Especially in Christian communities, it can be easy to merely say we are pro-life. But each of us can seek the Holy Spirit's guidance in asking what actions we can take in the present moment.

Jesus is moved to heal the paralytic by the faith of his friends. After seeing the large crowd gathered, they could have turned away. Instead, their compassion for their friend breaks through the barriers before them. They don't make excuses. They don't wait for a more convenient time. They find a way to bring the paralytic to Jesus—to heal their friend.

We, too, must break through the barriers we face, whether internal or external, to reach those mothers who are alone and afraid. We need to storm the gates of heaven with constant prayer and match our prayer with our action. We must pray and act with faith in our Lord's promise: "Where two or three are gathered together in my name, there am I in the midst of them."

Prayer:

Lord, your love is always the same and somehow always new. Your love is creative. Guide my steps, prompt my conversations, and help me to know how to reach expectant mothers contemplating an abortion. Help me to believe that you can and will work miracles through my faith.

DAY 18

Intention:
For the grace to respond with kindness and patience to those who oppose us.

Scripture:
"But to you who hear I say, love your enemies, do good to those who hate you, bless those who curse you, pray for those who mistreat you." —*Luke 6:27-28*

Reflection:
Christ calls us to a radical charity. He asks us to act with kindness and pray with sincerity for those who treat us unfairly. When we rely on human virtue alone, this radical call to charity is impossible, but through the grace of God, our hearts are transformed, and we can see even our enemies with the eyes of Christ.

God loves each person, including those most in need of his forgiveness and healing. He calls us to do the same.

The enemy will try to deceive us with the falsehood that loving those who oppose us is a betrayal of our beliefs. Yet it is only in acting with kindness and patience toward our opposition that we provide a space for the true conversion of minds and hearts.

Many people defend abortion out of ignorance and a misguided attempt to help others. It is up to us to appeal to the universal search for good to lead others to the truth.

Saint Augustine once said, "You don't love in your enemies what they are, but what you would have them become by your prayers."

In 1975, two years after *Roe v. Wade* legalized abortion, a young doctor by the name of Beverly McMillan helped open the first abortion clinic in Mississippi. Around the same time, she met Barbara, who became a good friend. "It didn't take us long to figure out that she was a Christian and I was a heathen," Dr. McMillan joked. "She was just delightful. She would be a good poker player; she was asking me about my practice, and when I told her that I was getting ready to open this abortion clinic, she was horrified, but I couldn't tell it. But she went home after that and called up her best friend, and they made a covenant over the phone to pray for me." Six months later, Dr. McMillan gave her life to Christ. But it took two more years for her to stop performing abortions. All the while, Barbara was a steadfast friend, taking her to church, giving her books to borrow, and never passing judgment or condemnation.

One day after performing an abortion of a 12-week-old baby, she noticed the bicep muscle and thought about her youngest son showing off his muscles. "It was just a God moment, a Holy Spirit moment." She realized, "Oh! If I'd left this alone, this child would have been as beautiful as mine."

Dr. McMillan's conversion began with one faithful friend. She has since become one of the biggest pro-life doctors and advocates in the state of Mississippi, helping thousands of mothers bring new life into this world. It all started with one friend who saw the good in her and didn't give up on God's power to transform even the hardest of hearts.

Prayer:

Lord, you showed friendship to the sinners and outcasts. You have been merciful in offering friendship to me. I long for true friendship with you and a Christ-centered friendship with those who need me. Let me show your kindness to those who fight against the right to life. Let me be understanding of their misguided intentions and own experiences. Let me be a bridge over which people may cross to your truth, goodness, and love.

DAY 19

Intention:

For every woman suffering from the grief and guilt of having an abortion.

Scripture:

"A woman of Samaria came to draw water. Jesus said to her, 'Give me a drink.'" —*John 4:7*

Reflection:

The Samaritan woman probably didn't expect to meet anyone at the well, let alone the Messiah. The Gospel of John includes an important detail that gives us insight into her encounter with Christ, stating that "it was about noon."

Typically, women did not go to the well in the middle of the day. They made the journey either early in the morning or in the evening to avoid the hottest part of the day. This Samaritan woman, however, is an outcast—scorned by other women for her adultery and isolated from society—so she goes to the well when she will almost certainly be alone.

There, she meets a man unlike any other person she's ever encountered. Jesus speaks to her without judgment or discrimination. He breaks the norms of the time and shows her respect by inviting her to draw water from the well. He reveals to her that he is the Messiah and that he has come to offer eternal life to all those who believe, regardless of their race, background, or history.

The great American evangelist Billy Graham once said: "You will be forgiven as if you had never sinned." Christ does not erase the Samaritan woman's past, but he recasts it in the light of his grace. He offers this same forgiveness to all who will accept it.

Many women who undergo an abortion feel a deep sense of regret afterward. Leading voices in our culture are so determined to tell women that abortion is good that they fail to acknowledge the real experiences of women who suffer such trauma. Because of this, many women feel they have no place to turn. The guilt and shame can cause some women to feel as though their past is too big for God to forgive.

Christ comes to save the sinners, the marginalized, and the lonely. He extends his mercy toward all persons who mourn their pasts, inviting them into the fullness of life just as he invites the Samaritan woman to receive the living water for which she thirsts— the same living water that is available to all of us today, no matter our mistakes. No sin is too big for God to forgive, no wound is too deep for God to heal, and no regret is beyond God's infinite mercy.

Prayer:

Heavenly Father, we pray in a special way for all women who have experienced an abortion. We ask that you draw these women close to your healing heart. Help us all to recognize our deep thirst for the living water that only you can offer, and give us the courage to invite others to the well of your forgiveness. Amen.

DAY 20

Intention:

For the fruit of these 40 days of prayer and fasting.

Scripture:

"But when you fast, anoint your head and wash your face, so that you may not appear to others to be fasting, except to your Father who is hidden. And your Father who sees what is hidden will repay you." —*Matthew 6:17-18*

Reflection:

It is natural to want others to notice when we do something good. It is human to desire affirmation. Yet Jesus calls his disciples to resist the temptation to draw attention to their sacrifices. He encourages us to serve as witnesses in a different way. By keeping our prayers and sacrifices hidden, we allow God to work in our hearts so that we become more and more detached from earthly comfort and security. Living with a spirit of sacrifice helps us to become more free to love.

Saint Mother Teresa of Calcutta is often remembered for her reflection on the transformative power of prayer: "I used to believe that prayer changes things, but now I know that prayer changes us, and we change things."

This brief statement is a striking reminder of the power of prayer. Jesus calls us to be prophets of joy who share his love with a weary world. Throughout these 40 days of prayer and fasting for life, we ask that God might change our hearts so that we can transform our culture into one that promotes the sacredness of life, from the moment of conception until natural death.

Jesus's instruction to combine the private habit of prayer with the life of joyful witness gives us a lens through which to view these 40 days, always trusting that God will not forget our hidden sacrifices.

We can look forward to the day in heaven when we might know the many lives saved through our prayers. Until then, we hold on to the promise that God will work more miracles than we can see through our quiet, steadfast prayer and fasting.

Prayer:

Heavenly Father, we ask for humility in our prayer and fasting. Help us to place you at the center of our lives so that others will come to know you through our words and deeds. As we continue through these 40 days, help us to listen to your voice, act in accord with your will, and trust in the power of prayer even when we don't always see the fruits on earth. Amen.

DAY 21

Intention:

That God will help all those struggling with doubts.

Scripture:

"Then the boy's father cried out, 'I do believe, help my unbelief!'" —*Mark 9:24*

Reflection:

Our work in the pro-life movement requires constant faith: faith in God's plan, in Christ's real presence on this earth, in the work of the Holy Spirit, and faith that we are building up the kingdom of God through our witness.

At times, however, it can be difficult not to give in to feelings of doubt. These feelings can arise for everyone: expectant parents, people on the front lines of pro-life activism, and others wrestling with their belief in God and questioning the sanctity of every life.

Especially in moments of uncertainty, Christ calls us to ask him for greater faith. When the father of a boy who is "possessed by a mute spirit" approaches Jesus in the Gospel of Mark, Christ implores him to have hope in God. "Everything is possible to one who has faith," Jesus tells the father.

After Christ performs a miracle to save the boy, his disciples ask why they were unable to cast out the mute spirit themselves. Jesus replies, "This kind can only come out through prayer."

He saves the boy not to prove his omnipotence, but rather to show that all things are possible through prayer. The Lord calls us to partake in his healing power by turning to him during moments of strife and reaffirming our faith when it's most difficult for us to trust in God's plan.

As we continue these 40 days of prayer, we ask God to strengthen our own faith so that our lives will be powerful witnesses for all those who are facing doubts about God and the sanctity of life.

Prayer:

Lord, we ask that you might grant every person struggling with doubts the reassurance that you are with them. We ask that you might work in the hearts of men and women who question your existence. We pray that more people will come to believe that you are the source of all strength and the summit of all hope. And we ask you to help us to trust that through your work in our lives, we can build up a culture that recognizes the dignity of every person. Amen.

DAY 22

Intention:

That God would multiply the fruits of 40 Days for Life.

Scripture:

"There is a boy here who has five barley loaves and two fish; but what good are these for so many?" —*John 6:9*

Reflection:

Our Lord is aware of our needs, our wants, and our deficiencies, and he will never be out-done in generosity.

On our own, we can often feel limited in our ability to meet the needs of others.

In the Gospel of John, as thousands of people grow hungry after a long day of lis-tening to Jesus, the apostles experience these feelings of limitation firsthand. With only five barley loaves and two fish, they can't see any plausible solution. "Two hundred days' wages worth of food would not be enough for each of them to have a little," says Philip. Christ's disciple Andrew agrees: "What good are these for so many?"

Though his disciples cannot grasp what he's about to do, Jesus instructs them to have the 5,000 sit down. Despite their lack of faith, he gives the disciples a chance to participate in the miracle he is about to perform, even if only in a seemingly small way.

After the crowd sat down, "Jesus took the loaves, gave thanks, and distributed them to those who were reclining, and also as much of the fish as they wanted."

Like the disciples, sometimes we find ourselves feeling like there is no way we can reach all those who need the bread of life. In a culture that often worships personal autonomy over God, our own prayers and actions can feel insufficient in defending the dignity of life. But this passage reminds us that Christ can multiply our efforts, small though they may be.

The extraordinary miracle of the loaves and fishes foreshadows the miracle of the Last Supper. Christ gives us his body and blood in the bread and wine.

Upon reflecting on this gift of Holy Communion, Saint Josemaría Escrivá wrote, "He offers himself to us as nourishment in the most natural and ordinary way. Love has been awaiting us for almost two thousand years. That's a long time and yet it's not, for when you are in love time flies."

Christ is with us. He gives us the strength we don't have. He teaches us to depend more and more on him. Our humble offerings can reach the whole world, not through their own merit, but through Christ, the Bread of Life.

Prayer:

Lord, you multiplied the meager offering of one boy to feed a hungry crowd. Please do the same with our humble prayers. Multiply the fruits of these 40 days. Use our own resources to glorify your name. Grant us the humility to know our limitations, the wisdom to turn to you in moments of distress, and the grace to carry out your will with trust and courage. Amen.

DAY 23

Intention:

That mothers who feel abandoned would know that God will not leave them.

Scripture:

"They woke him and said to him, 'Teacher, do you not care that we are perishing?'"
—*Mark 4:38*

Reflection:

Sometimes the storms of life rage on in ways that do not make sense, rising suddenly or lasting far longer than we expect. Mothers who face pressure from friends or family to abort, who struggle to make ends meet, or who feel isolated in their motherhood may ask God the same question the disciples did: "Do you not care?"

Jesus and his disciples embark on their journey after a long day of public ministry. Earlier in the same chapter, Jesus shares with his disciples that he is the Messiah. But as Jesus sleeps through the storm, the disciples begin to doubt that he will save them. When the disciples wake him up in panic, Jesus answers them: "Why are you terrified? Do you not yet have faith?"

Nothing is beyond God's control. Though Christ slept, he did not forget his friends. Rather, he let the storm test their faith. They had heard Jesus' words earlier that day, but had they truly believed them? In our own lives, do we believe that Jesus is the Messiah, or do the storms of life cause us to doubt?

Faith is not a solitary act. It is a journey of friendship to experience God's care for each of us through the people he places in our lives. As Psalm 139 declares, we are "fearfully and wonderfully made," and our father in heaven cares for us far more than he does the sparrows or the lilies of the field.

We are the ones who turn away from God, who start to think he doesn't care, and who begin to lose faith. God is always by our side. He lets us endure stormy waters to grow in faith, but he is with us in the boat waiting for us to call upon his name.

Prayer:

Dear Lord, I know that you are always with me and that you work all things for good. When the truth of your perpetual presence is difficult to grasp, give me the grace to remember that you are a good and gracious father in every circumstance. Help us to speak this truth to those around us. In a special way, we ask you to wrap mothers who feel abandoned in your mantle. Amen.

DAY 24

Intention:

For every family who has lost a child, born or unborn.

Scripture:

"And Jesus wept." —*John 11:35*

Reflection:

Jesus was a strong man: a carpenter, a teacher, the son of God. Consider how he wept. Imagine the sight of the Messiah breaking down in tears at the death of his friend. His tears are raw and vulnerable.

The enemy will try to convince us that God wants us to suffer. He will show us all the evil that exists and say, "Where is he?" But the enemy lies. Jesus did not merely shed a solitary tear for Lazarus. He wept, and then he brought his friend back from the dead.

God knows that the battle has already been won, that the victory is his. However, this does not stop him from being with us in our daily sorrows. It does not stop him from listening to our cries and comforting the brokenhearted.

Jesus wept from an overflowing heart. He wept because he lost his friend; because Martha and Mary grieved the loss of their brother. Jesus wept, knowing full well that he was moments away from entering the tomb and raising a dead man to life. He wept, not because he did not know what was to come, but because he loved.

Sorrow is not evidence of a lack of faith, but a sign of love. A parent who mourns the loss of a child can find comfort in the assurance that Jesus weeps with them.

Charity invites us to share in the sufferings of others. How often do we close our eyes to the pain of another because we don't want to complicate our lives, we don't want to risk opening the floodgates of our own emotions? How often do we distance ourselves from a grieving friend because we fear the demands of love?

An unborn child in pain weeps, but we cannot hear her cry. We must be her tears and her voice. Let us open our hearts with compassion for grieving parents and their lost children, to accompany them in carrying their burden. Let us weep as Jesus wept, with the faith that even death bows to the feet of Christ.

Prayer:

Lord, grant us the courage to weep. Let our tears mingle with yours and with parents who have lost a child. Grant them the solace of your peace, the confidence that their son or daughter is interceding for them in heaven, and the hope that they will be reunited in eternity. Amen.

DAY 25

Intention:

For parents facing difficult pregnancies.

Scripture:

"And Jesus went with them, but when he was only a short distance from the house, the centurion sent friends to tell him, 'Lord, do not trouble yourself, for I am not worthy to have you enter under my roof. Therefore, I did not consider myself worthy to come to you; but say the word and let my servant be healed.'"
—*Luke 7:6-7*

Reflection:

The centurion was a pagan in the eyes of the Jewish people. The presence of Jesus, whom the centurion clearly recognized as a holy and sacred man, provoked a sentiment of shame evident in his words: "Do not trouble yourself, for I am not worthy." What a bittersweet phrase. How often do we feel that our problems are not worthy of our Lord?

"To love at all is to be vulnerable," C. S. Lewis wrote in *The Four Loves*. "Love anything and your heart will be wrung and possibly broken. If you want to make sure of keeping it intact you must give it to no one, not even an animal. Wrap it carefully round with hobbies and little luxuries; avoid all entanglements. Lock it up safe in the casket or coffin of your selfishness. But in that casket, safe, dark, motionless, airless, it will change. It will not be broken; it will become unbreakable, impenetrable, irredeemable."

In the city of Cardiff, Wales, one couple was told that their unborn baby would not survive a pregnancy due to severe health complications. They feared the seemingly inevitable loss of their child and sought an abortion. But through the grace of God, a 40 Days for Life prayer warrior was standing outside the clinic and encouraged the couple to put the life of their child in God's hands.

Years later, the father brought his young daughter to the same vigil site to meet the 40 Days for Life prayer warriors. She was a beautiful, healthy little girl. Those parents made themselves vulnerable to love, even though the conditions of their daughter's life were beyond their control. God blessed their faith and saved their daughter despite the seemingly impossible odds.

Jesus waits at the door of our souls, eager for us to invite him in, to hand our troubles over to his loving care. The centurion did not feel worthy of meeting Christ, but his faith was enough for Christ to grant his request. May we have the courage to invite Christ into our lives, to surrender everything to him, and to find shelter in his most sacred wounds.

Prayer:

Dear Lord, I surrender my fear to your loving care. Give mothers and fathers the courage to invite you into their lives in good times and bad, and grant them the faith to place their children in your hands. Lead them to doctors who will give their children the very best chance to live. Amen.

DAY 26

Intention:

That pastors and priests would receive each person with the compassion of Christ.

Scripture:

"While he was still a long way off, his father caught sight of him, and was filled with compassion. He ran to his son, embraced him and kissed him." —*Luke 15:20*

Reflection:

A good pastor is like the father of the prodigal son: he welcomes every person who approaches the steps of the church with warmth and compassion. He is a messenger of God's mercy.

In the parable of the prodigal son, the father doesn't wait for his son to knock on his door. He runs toward his son, embraces him, and walks with him until they both reach home.

Pastors and laypeople alike can emulate this example not only by welcoming newcomers to their congregations, but also by inviting more to come. It can feel daunting to reach new people, but often it begins with small steps: inviting a neighbor over for a meal, talking to the person sitting next to us on a plane, thanking the cashier, or a host of other opportunities in the midst of our daily lives. When we are open to sharing God's love, Christ puts people in our path. In pro-life work, this accompaniment can be life-changing for women who are searching for answers.

As the body of Christ, we have a responsibility to build up our pastors. They serve a special role in the church by freely offering their lives to shepherd the faithful, but they cannot do this work alone. Though they take on the role of the father, they are also prodigal sons.

Henri Nouwen, a 20th-century Dutch priest and psychologist, reflected on the story of the prodigal son in relation to his own life: "God is looking into the distance for me, trying to find me, and longing to bring me home," Nouwen wrote.* "The question is not 'How am I to love God?' but 'How am I to let myself be loved by God?'"

This is the question for all people, since we are all called to be both forgiving fathers and repentant sons. Christ calls every Christian to spread the hope of the Gospel to those who are longing to hear his word—and he calls priests and pastors to live out this calling in a particular way. They need and deserve our prayers and support. Let us ask God how he wants us to encourage and thank the pastors in our communities.

Prayer:

Jesus, you have given us good pastors to lead your faithful. We thank you for their guidance and service, and we ask you to give them renewed strength. Help them to follow you with steadfast devotion. Guide their every action and give them the words to say to bring many people back to you. Amen.

---

*Henri J.M. Nouwen, *The Return of the Prodigal Son: A Story of Homecoming*

DAY 27

Intention:

That every person in the pro-life movement would treat each individual with love.

Scripture:

"I give you a new commandment: love one another. As I have loved you, so you also should love one another." —*John 13:34*

Reflection:

Jesus entered time to teach us how to love. His is not a mild or comfortable love, but one that brought him to be scourged, humiliated, and nailed to the wood of the cross. We cannot be fooled by any watered-down version of Christianity. To love as Christ did is to fully give of oneself.

The early Christians were said to be instantly recognizable by this love. Even in times of persecution, when they had to practice their faith in secret, the pagans would say, "These Christians, see how they love one another."

Christ puts each one of us in a specific time and place for a crucial, irreplaceable role. He relies on each of us to be "another Christ, Christ himself," as Gregory of Nyssa put it. In every encounter, we have the chance not only to be another Christ but also to see Christ in others.

In her *Story of a Soul*, Saint Therese of Lisieux recalled a particularly irritating sister with whom she lived. Everything this sister did was infuriating to Therese. Concerned that this would lead her to a lack of charity, Therese committed not only to hold her tongue, but also to go out of her way to be kind to this sister. Eventually, this sister approached Therese and asked her what it was that Therese liked about her. "Ah!" Saint Therese later wrote in her diary, "It was Jesus hidden in the depth of her soul who attracted me, Jesus, who makes the bitterest things sweet!"

Like Saint Therese, let us ask God to help us see his beloved son in each person we encounter, especially those who are hardest to love.

Prayer:

Dear Jesus, please instill in me a rich under-standing of your love so that I might share it with others. Grant me the courage to open my heart to others. Give me the grace to treat each person as I would treat you. Amen.

DAY 28

Intention:

For expectant mothers beginning to doubt that God will provide.

Scripture:

"Peter got out of the boat and began to walk on the water toward Jesus. But when he saw how [strong] the wind was he became frightened; and, beginning to sink, he cried out, 'Lord, save me!'" —*Matthew 14:29-30*

Reflection:

When Peter jumped into the stormy sea, his eyes were fixed on Jesus. The moment he broke his gaze, he began to sink.

Peter had every reason to doubt. In the dark of night, he stepped into the middle of thrashing waves. No man had ever walked on water. Why would it be possible now?

Yet Jesus calls Peter to have faith beyond the realities he could see.

Life is full of uncertainty. Naturally, we want to wait for the perfect circumstances to respond to God's promptings. But the perfect circumstances never come. Peter shows us again and again that God does not demand perfection. All he asks is that we step out of the boat of conformity and wade into the unknown to follow him.

Expectant mothers often confront many moments of darkness—from fears about how they will provide, who will care for their babies while they are working, and whether they will be able to give their children a better life than they had. But Jesus never leaves them alone. Let us strengthen them with our friendship and prayers.

It is easy to find false comfort in the illusion of control rather than laying our problems in God's hands. To surrender everything to God—the past, present, and future—is to embrace hope over despair. The very nature of motherhood and fatherhood requires this heroic surrender to God.

Prayer:

Thank you, Lord, for my doubt, which allows me to practice faith. Hear my prayer for expectant mothers. Give them the courage to walk in faith. Help them to see the nobility of their motherhood. Through the storms of life, keep them close to you and comfort them in the safety of your arms. Amen.

DAY 29

Intention:

To thank God for all the mothers whose lives have been changed and babies who have been saved through 40 Days for Life.

Scripture:

"And one of them, realizing he had been healed, returned, glorifying God in a loud voice." —*Luke 17:15*

Reflection:

Blessed Solanus Casey, a Capuchin priest, once offered a dying girl this advice: "Thank God ahead of time." The prayer of gratitude is the most trusting prayer.

As we ask God to continue to bless our work, we thank him for the many miracles he has already worked. More than 23,000 babies have been saved through the prayers and work of 40 Days for Life volunteers.

The ten lepers were already well on their way when they realized they were healed. We don't know how long they walked before their sores disappeared, but it was long enough that they could no longer see Christ. They quickly forgot the one who healed them—all but one leper who turned back to express his thanks.

The leper finds Jesus, whose sadness is audible when he says: "Ten were cleansed, were they not? Where are the other nine?" Christ didn't need the credit or the praise. He wanted the nine other lepers to recognize the source of their healing—to be transformed not only in body but in soul.

The grateful leper received an additional gift. Jesus says, "Your faith has saved you." Christ not only cured him of his physical ailment, he forgave his sins and offered him eternal life. Just like the leper who returned, we want to turn back to God again and again, thanking him for the ways in which he saves us from our sins.

Every victory belongs to God. It is never too late for God to work miracles, and it is never too early to thank him for them.

Prayer:

Dear Lord, thank you for the innumerable babies and mothers who have been saved from abortion through 40 Days for Life. And thank you in advance for the lives that will be changed through this campaign. Work in our own hearts so that we might see every circumstance as a chance to grow closer to you and to express our thanksgiving for your faithfulness. Amen.

Day 30

Intention:

For children who are adopted or in foster care.

Scripture:

"And whoever receives one child such as this in my name receives me. ... See that you do not despise one of these little ones, for I say to you that their angels in heaven always look upon the face of my heavenly Father." —*Matthew 18:5,10*

Reflection:

In an address to adoptive families, Saint John Paul II said, "To adopt a child is a great work of love. When it is done, much is given, but much is also received. It is a true exchange of gifts."

To adopt or foster a child is to imitate God's fatherly love—to care for another's child as one's own. It is a calling that changes the lives of the children the parents welcome into their homes.

We must pray for every foster and adoptive family and for every child in need of a loving family. Tragically, too many children in foster care have not been treated with the kindness and care they deserve. We need Christian families to open their hearts to children in the broken foster system.

Though not every family is called to foster or adopt children, we are all called to care for children in the ways that we can. Whether by volunteering as a mentor to a child in need, helping at an after-school program, or donating to faith-based adoption and foster care organizations, each of us can look for opportunities to follow the words of the Gospel: to receive one child is to receive Christ.

God promises that his angels are watching over his children. Let us pray for God's protection upon every child and for his guidance to help couples discerning whether they are called to the selfless gift of adoption.

Prayer:

Lord, keep every child free from harm. Especially in moments of despair, help them to sense the presence of your angels watching over them. Provide a loving home for every child in need, and strengthen and sustain adoptive and foster parents to imitate your fatherly care. Amen.

DAY 31

Intention:

For mothers who have suffered a miscarriage.

Scripture:

"Jesus told him, 'Have sight; your faith has saved you.'" —*Luke 18:42*

Reflection:

The pain of a miscarriage is magnified by the fact that many mourning mothers suffer in secret. Couples grieving such a loss need support, prayers, and time to heal. This emotional and physical healing is not a "return to normal," but rather a process of integrating the reality of grief into one's life.

The Gospel is filled with stories of miraculous healings. Jesus, who is the Divine Physician and the Prince of Peace, draws all things into the fullness of life. He heals the woman with a hemorrhage, restores Jairus's daughter to life, cleanses lepers, and opens the eyes of the blind.

When the blind man hears that Jesus is passing by on the road to Jericho, he cries out, "Jesus, Son of David, have pity on me!" Jesus hears him and approaches. The blind man asks, "Lord, please let me see." Jesus responds, "Have sight; your faith has saved you."

Mothers mourning a miscarriage often find themselves plagued by the same kinds of questions that the blind man may have asked before meeting Jesus: Why did this happen to me? Did I do something wrong? Will this darkness ever end?

Receiving the gift of sight did not erase the years of blindness the man in the Gospel endured. But after being healed, it's easy to imagine that the blind man had a renewed sense of gratitude for beauty in the world and compassion toward others suffering from the same affliction. The proper response to healing, after all, is to pour out what Christ has given us so that others might also be healed.

Some mothers who have miscarried have used their loss to serve others suffering the same grief. When John and Sara Rogers miscarried, they felt isolated and unsure of what to do next. Eager to help other couples navigate the same experience, they created a website called Catholic Miscarriage Support, which offers both practical and spiritual guidance for couples who have lost a child through miscarriage.

In the depths of grief, God asks us to have the faith of the blind man—to see not with human vision but with supernatural sight, filled with the hope that one day parents will meet their sons and daughters in heaven.

Prayer:

Dear Lord, give us the courage to pray for miraculous healings of body and soul. Extend your mercy to mothers and fathers who have experienced miscarriage. Grant them the peace of your son, and help them to rest in the assurance that they will one day be reunited with their precious children. Amen.

DAY 32

Intention:

For the desire to serve the needs of others.

Scripture:

"Then he poured water into a basin and began to wash the disciples' feet and dry them with the towel around his waist." *—John 13:5*

Reflection:

The Son of God, the King of the universe, takes on the role of a household servant when he washes the feet of his disciples. On the eve of his passion, Jesus serves his disciples on his knees.

The scene illustrates what Paul said in Philippians: "Though he was in the form of God, he did not regard equality with God something to be grasped. Rather, he emptied himself, taking the form of a slave."

The disciples are imperfect. Judas will betray Jesus mere hours later, Peter will deny his master three times, and only John will be brave enough to stand at the foot of the cross. Yet Jesus encounters his friends in the mess of their daily lives. He accepts them as they are, even as he calls them to deeper holiness.

We serve others to serve Christ. At times our efforts will go unnoticed. The work will be thankless and unglamorous. But we put others' needs above our own out of an outpouring of gratitude for what Christ has done for us. Service is not an investment; it is a gift freely given without expecting anything in return.

As Oswald Chambers put it, "If our devotion is to the cause of humanity, we will be quickly defeated and broken-hearted, since we will often be confronted with a great deal of ingratitude from other people. But if we are motivated by our love for God, no amount of ingratitude will be able to hinder us from serving one another."

Jesus wasn't afraid to wash the feet of sinners. If God is so generous to such an undeserving world, how much more generous should we be to him?

Prayer:

God, stir up in us the desire to serve as you serve. Grant us the discernment to understand your will for our lives, to use our gifts for your glory, and to love our neighbor well. When we feel that our efforts are in vain, remind us that we do everything for your glory, not for our own fame or recognition. Amen.

DAY 33

Intention:

To draw closer to Jesus during this 40-day journey.

Scripture:

"When he returned to his disciples he found them asleep. He said to Peter, 'So you could not keep watch with me for one hour? Watch and pray that you may not undergo the test. The spirit is willing, but the flesh is weak.'"
—*Matthew 26:40-41*

Reflection:

Christ's agony in the garden teaches us how to suffer. Since Jesus was fully God and fully man, this scene teaches us that fear of pain is not a sin. It is an invitation to rely more fully on our Lord, who experienced this same anguish.

Jesus' agony in the garden was so severe that he underwent a rare medical phenomenon in which stress induces the sweating of blood. Luke, who was a physician, includes this detail to portray the depths of Christ's anguish. What a moving detail of Christ's humanity: even our savior wasn't immune to the physical reaction of mental anxiety.

In the garden of Gethsemane, Jesus does not ask Peter to say or do anything; he simply asks for him to be with him. This is the mark of true friendship—to be able to sit in silence with another, to share an understanding without words, and to accompany a friend in moments of distress. It can seem like an impossible task to help our friends in need, but often the greatest thing we can do is pray for them, offer silent sacrifices, and reassure them with our presence.

Christ longs for intimate friendship with us. Saint John Vianney once asked a peasant man sitting in a church what he was praying about. "Nothing," the man replied. "I look at him and he looks at me."

This peasant man was profoundly wise in his simplicity. He knew that he didn't have to prove his goodness to God, he didn't have to utter poetic phrases. He simply wanted to be with our Lord, to stay awake with him, to keep watch for an hour.

During these final days of this 40-day challenge, it is easy to want to give in little ways—to lessen our sacrifices or defer our time of prayer until suddenly we are in bed and we realize it's too late. Yet God is offering us an opportunity to stay close to him when he needs our prayers the most.

Do not leave Jesus alone in the garden. Keep watch with him, comfort him, and find peace in his loving gaze. In so doing, we can bring others to the garden of Christ and abandon ourselves to the will of our loving father.

Prayer:

Most sweet Jesus, my heart aches for your suffering and loneliness in the garden of Gethsemane. Let me never fall asleep again when you so lovingly ask for my company. When I feel alone and afraid, remind me that you are with me and that you feel the pain that I feel. Keep me close to you on this 40-day journey and strengthen me through your blood and tears.

DAY 34

Intention:

To accept the opportunity to suffer with Christ.

Scripture:

"As they led him away they took hold of a certain Simon, a Cyrenian, who was coming in from the county; and after laying the cross on him, they made him carry it behind Jesus."
—*Luke 23:26*

Reflection:

In one of the greatest mysteries of our faith, Christ freely chooses to die for us. On the way to Calvary, Simon of Cyrene joins in Christ's suffering, bearing with him the indescribable weight of the cross.

In reflecting on this scene, St. Josemaría wrote, "At times the Cross appears without our looking for it: it is Christ who is seeking us out. And if by chance, before this unexpected

Cross which, perhaps, is therefore more difficult to understand, your heart were to show repugnance…don't give it consolations, and filled with a noble compassion, when it asks for them, say to it slowly, as one speaking in confidence: 'Heart: heart on the Cross! Heart on the Cross!'"

Our Lord is stumbling through a hostile crowd: an entire city jeering at him, soldiers pushing him, already half dead, onto the ground beneath their feet. With few exceptions, onlookers find entertainment in his agony.

Where are Jesus's friends? Where are those he had healed? Where are the thousands who just days before had laid palms at his feet in a procession fit for a king? Why are the soldiers forced to choose a stranger to lighten his load?

Where are we in Christ's suffering? Do we too flee the scene?

Simon of Cyrene does not plan on helping Jesus. He isn't a follower of the Messiah. At first, he likely resents the soldiers forcing him to assist a stranger. But the very face of Christ is enough to spark a conversion of heart. Jesus allows Simon to share in his load not to punish him, but to redeem him.

Christ invites us to be modern-day Simons of Cyrene: to get to know Jesus by sharing in his suffering. United to Christ, the cross is a joyful burden, an easy yoke. It marks the difference between meaningless pain and noble sacrifice. By uniting our sorrows to Christ's, we participate in his redemption of all of mankind and bind ourselves to a purpose beyond this world.

Prayer:

Lord, teach us how to suffer alongside you. Grant us the joy of your company under the wood of the cross. Grant us the strength of Simon to help you on your way. We unite every tired step and discouraging defeat to your sacrifice for the redemption of all humanity. Amen.

DAY 35

Intention:

For all those who seek to advance abortion worldwide.

Scripture:

"Father, forgive them, they know not what they do." —*Luke 23:34*

Reflection:

Every abortion is an act of violence. We must hate the sin, but love the sinner.

Most people who fiercely advocate for abortion do so because they mistakenly believe it will bring greater freedom to women. Often blinded by pain in their own lives, abortion advocates discount the tiny life in the womb. It is tempting to disdain those who want to end human life, but Christ teaches us how to respond to violence and hate.

During his final moments on earth, it would have been easy for Christ to despise his persecutors. Yet after being brutally scourged, mocked, and crucified, Jesus does not condemn. Instead, he begs for his father's mercy upon those who stripped him of everything.

Today, most abortion activists believe they are acting righteously to help vulnerable mothers. But violence never brings healing. Some of the greatest advocates for life are people who previously fought for abortion until they saw the evil practice for what it is: the murder of an innocent life that inflicts irreversible harm on mother and baby.

In truth, abortion advocates seek a good, though their intention is misplaced. They misunderstand freedom, thinking that the death of her child can liberate the mother, when in reality it does the reverse.

When Pope John Paul II addressed World Youth Day in 2000, he explained people's search for fulfillment this way: "It is Jesus in fact that you seek when you dream of happiness; he is waiting for you when nothing else you find satisfies you; he is the beauty to which you are so attracted; it is he who provokes you with that thirst for fullness that will not let you settle for compromise; it is he who urges you to shed the masks of a false life; it is he who reads in your hearts your most genuine choices, the choices that others try to stifle."

We can hope, pray, and work for the day when every abortion activist opens his or her heart to the truth and joins our movement to give every woman the freedom to choose life. Until that day, we ask God to forgive them, for "they know not what they do."

Prayer:

Lord, we pray that you might help us to look with mercy upon those who seek to advance the evil of abortion. We ask that you lead them to a sincere conversion of heart. And we pray that you might help them to see the grace imbued in every soul and embrace the beauty that every child brings to the world. Amen.

DAY 36

Intention:

For individuals who have suffered from abuse and trafficking.

Scripture:

"When Jesus saw his mother and the disciple there whom he loved, he said to his mother, 'Woman, behold, your son.'" —*John 19:26*

Reflection:

Mary watched her son endure the most unthinkable pain. While the world will never understand all that survivors of sex trafficking and abuse have endured, Christ does. He is grieved by the injustice done by evil perpetrators.

Each person is made with the utmost dignity and destiny for the highest good, and sex crimes wound the dignity of a human person in a particularly grievous way.

Tragically, as many as 300,000 women and more than 100,000 children are estimated to be victims of human trafficking every year in the United States. These statistics are staggering and deeply saddening.

The secrecy, shame, and loneliness in abusive situations can multiply the pain. Although the injury of abuse may never disappear, brave survivors can find healing in the loving arms of God, who promises to be close to the brokenhearted.

Let us pray that every survivor will find refuge in Christ, whose compassion is a salve for the deepest wounds.

Our prayers to end abortion must be inseparable from our prayers to end abuse and trafficking, for abortion is a link in the chain of human abuse. Abortion only further harms victims while allowing abusers to perpetuate violence.

Many churches and Christian organizations have been on the front lines of the efforts to stop the evils of human trafficking and provide a safe haven for survivors. Although ending this modern form of slavery can feel impossible, nothing is impossible with God.

Through Christ, we can help survivors build a new life of freedom and dignity.

There is no wound too deep, no scar too hidden, and no knot too tangled for the redeeming mercy of God.

Prayer:

Most loving God, please help the victims of abuse, trafficking, and broken relationships. Provide them with immediate and permanent safety from danger. In your loving arms, heal them from injuries—physical, psychological, and spiritual. Lead them to the best sources of support and healing. Bring comfort to all victims of abuse, and help children conceived in abusive situations to know they are loved by you. Amen.

DAY 37

Intention:

That we would help all those who have participated in an abortion know that it's never too late to ask for God's forgiveness.

Scripture:

"Jesus, remember me when you come into your kingdom." —*Luke 23:42*

Reflection:

As Jesus hangs, dying, on Mount Calvary, he suffers in the company of two criminals. Both had been convicted of theft, and they wonder at the innocent man in their company. One criminal mocks Jesus, asking, "Are you not the Messiah? Save yourself and us."

But the other thief recognizes that Jesus is innocent and makes a bold proclamation of faith: "Jesus, remember me when you come into your kingdom."

The reactions of these two thieves illustrate the reactions that we, as sinners, can have to Jesus. He is always with us, but we can either reject his presence or find freedom in his forgiveness. We can form habits that rely on our own will or on God's plan for us. Christ waits for us just as he waits for the repentant thief to cry out to him.

Abortion is a grave sin, but nothing is beyond the power of God's forgiveness. At every moment, God calls those who have in some way participated in an abortion to turn back to him and ask for forgiveness. Even at his execution, moments away from death, the second thief was not too late to receive Christ's everlasting redemption.

Former abortionist Dr. John Bruchalski is a witness to the forgiveness that is possible through God's grace. Dr. Bruchalski specialized as an OB-GYN because he wanted to help women to live healthy lives. When he was in medical school, he learned how to perform abortions and continued to do so throughout his residency. During one late-term abortion, he unintentionally delivered a baby weighing over one pound. By law, he had to send the baby to the neonatal unit. When he called the hospital, the doctor told him that he was treating the baby like a tumor instead of a patient. That was the last abortion he performed.

"The scales fell from my eyes," Dr. Bruchalski recalled years later. He started a pro-life OB-GYN practice that has served thousands of women and children.

The forgiveness and healing that Dr. Bruchalski experienced are available to every doctor, nurse, and person involved in the abortion industry. It's never too late. Like the repentant thief, all people can express their contrition and open themselves to the mercy of Christ. They can find consolation in Jesus's dying promise: "Amen, I say to you, today you will be with me in Paradise."

Prayer:

God, we ask that those who have participated in abortion will know that your mercy does not expire. Help us to forgive as you do so that others might come to understand the dignity of every human life, including their own. Convert the hearts of abortionists. May they experience your forgiveness as Dr. Bruchalski and so many others have. Amen.

DAY 38

Intention:

To rest in the hope that God's plan is bigger than our own.

Scripture:

"On the first day of the week, Mary of Magdala came to the tomb early in the morning while it was still dark, and saw the stone removed from the tomb." —*John 20:1*

Reflection:

The light of the Easter morning washes out the darkness through which Mary Magdalene walks. As soon as she sees the empty tomb, the Gospel of John tells us that she runs to Peter and John and tells them the news. They run back to the tomb. They see the burial clothes rolled up, and Jesus is nowhere to be found.

The disciples leave, but Mary stays outside the tomb weeping. Two angels descend and ask her why she weeps. "They have taken my Lord, and I don't know where they laid him," Mary replies.

Jesus appears and asks her, "Whom are you looking for?" Mary doesn't recognize him. She begs the man, "Sir, if you carried him away, tell me where you laid him, and I will take him."

Jesus utters her name, and Mary suddenly knows she's speaking to her master, the resurrected Lord. Her heart is set aflame with wonder and relief, but most of all love—she has found our Lord. He makes himself known to Mary Magdalene first, who is the first to seek him out on Easter morning. Mary sees and believes and her fears are cast away. Her life is changed once again and her gratitude is renewed.

Often we, like Mary, wonder where our Lord has gone. We doubt his presence in our lives and question his plan because it is not going according to our own.

Even when we know that our own plan is faltering, we struggle to abandon our lives to God because we are afraid of what he might ask of us. We are afraid to step into the empty tomb. But just as Mary Magdalene makes an act of faith in the darkness, so too are we called to run to Christ in times of trial. No matter how great our worries, Christ's plan is always greater than our own designs.

Our vision is small, but God is infinite. As Romans 8:28 promises, "We know that all things work for good for those who love God, who are called according to his purpose."

His plans are not only good, they are perfectly designed to help us reach eternity. In his famous *Four Quartets,* the 20th-century poet T. S. Eliot reflected on this homesickness for heaven:

"We shall not cease from exploration
And the end of all our exploring
Will be to arrive where we started
And know the place for the first time."

Our home—the place from which we came and long to return—is in God himself.

Prayer:

Father, you never fail. Time and time again you have triumphed: with the overturn of *Roe v. Wade,* with the conversion of abortion doctors, with the courageous mothers who have chosen life, and with the countless babies saved against all odds. Why, then, do I doubt that you will help us now? I believe that you will make abortion unthinkable in this country. I believe that you will help us empower women to choose life. I believe that no setback is permanent. I believe that you have a plan far greater than anything I could ever conceive on my own. I surrender the past, present, and future to you. Amen.

Day 39

Intention:

That more women receive an ultrasound and choose life.

Scripture:

"Then he said to Thomas, 'Put your finger here and see my hands, and bring your hand and put it into my side, and do not be unbelieving, but believe.' Thomas answered and said to him, 'My Lord and my God!'" —*John 20:27-28*

Reflection:

In this Gospel scene, Jesus uses sight to instill faith. When Thomas heard that his fellow disciples had seen Jesus, he said, "Unless I see the mark of the nails in his hands and put my finger into the nailmarks and put my hand into his side, I will not believe."

A week later, Jesus again appeared to his disciples. This time, Thomas was there. Jesus didn't have to prove anything to Thomas. He didn't have to prove that he had risen from the dead, that he was the same teacher Thomas had loved, or that he was the Messiah, the son of God. Yet Christ, in his magnanimity, gave the doubting disciple what he wanted. He offered his wounds for Thomas to touch with his own hands.

Just as Thomas believed after he saw Christ, God often uses the sight of an ultrasound to help mothers believe in the lives of their children.

It has been estimated that at least 60 percent of women considering abortion choose to carry their babies to term after having an ultrasound. There are innumerable stories of mothers whose hearts have melted after seeing their tiny children dance, blink, suck their thumbs, or leap in the womb. Mothers see that their unborn children are wholly alive and undeniably human.

In the past, technological limitations allowed abortionists to hide this scientific truth. Now, ultrasounds provide a window into the womb. Dr. Joseph Randall, a former abortion provider, explained that even abortion clinics recognize the power of the ultrasound: "They [the women] are never allowed to look at the ultrasound because we knew that if they so much as heard the heartbeat, they wouldn't want to have an abortion."*

The very heart of the unborn child beats in protest against his or her unjust death.

Thousands of pregnancy centers around the country provide free ultrasounds to empower women to see the life growing inside them. Every woman deserves to see her baby. The power of an ultrasound image proves that women want to choose life, especially when they see the living, breathing, moving babies inside their wombs.

Prayer:

Dear Jesus, thank you for the ways that science helps us to better see and know your creation. Please lead every expectant mother to a place that will enable her to see her child with an ultrasound. Grant her the simplicity to see the humanity in her womb and the courage to protect it. Amen.

---

* "Pro-Choice 1990: Skeletons in the Closet," *New Dimensions*, October 1990

DAY 40

Intention:

To carry the light of Christ wherever we go.

Scripture:

"Go, therefore, and make disciples of all nations, baptizing them in the name of the Father, and of the Son, and of the Holy Spirit, teaching them to observe all that I have commanded you. And behold, I am with you always, until the end of the age."
—*Matthew 28:19-20*

Reflection:

What are we to do with the abundance of grace offered to us? The paradox of God's generosity lies in the fact that it multiplies when we share it with others.

Christ calls all Christians to bring the light of the Gospel to the world. The first Christians made harrowing journeys to Greece,

Rome, Macedonia, Asia, and beyond. They were met with hostility, skepticism, and persecution. Some were stoned, imprisoned, and fed to the lions in the area. Yet persecution did not stop Christ's followers from spreading the good news. Through their perseverance, thousands upon thousands came to know the one true God.

The Acts of the Apostles recounts the storm Paul endured in the middle of the sea while he was a prisoner: "Neither the sun nor the stars were visible for many days, and no small storm raged. Finally, all hope of our surviving was taken away." Paul urged his captors, "Keep up your courage; not one of you will be lost, only the ship."

Christ encourages us to do the same. Keep your courage. God is present through the difficulties. Even when it seems impossible to save every soul, even when it seems foolish to think that America will one day protect every human life, we must remember that with God nothing is impossible.

Without God we can do nothing. With God we can change the world. We can see the day when every child is protected and every family is cherished. We can make abortion a tragic injustice of the past. We can usher in a new era in our history that cherishes the divine gift of every life, from the moment of conception until natural death. If America leads, the world will follow.

Christ set us on a mission to save the souls of the lost. On this divine adventure, let us be aware of our own shortcomings and recklessly confident in Christ's power. Whatever grace God gives us, we must share it with others tenfold.

As the Gospel of Luke tells us, "Much will be required of the person entrusted with much, and still more will be demanded of the person entrusted with more."

The message is clear: Go.

Prayer:

God, you have given me more than I could possibly ask. Help me never stray from your presence, for it is you whom I long to share with everyone I encounter. Show your face through my humility, direct my steps, and let every word I speak be from you. You ascended to Heaven not to abandon us but to be with us. You sent the Holy Spirit to guide our actions. As we conclude this 40-day fast, pour forth your grace on us to carry your light to the ends of the world. Amen.